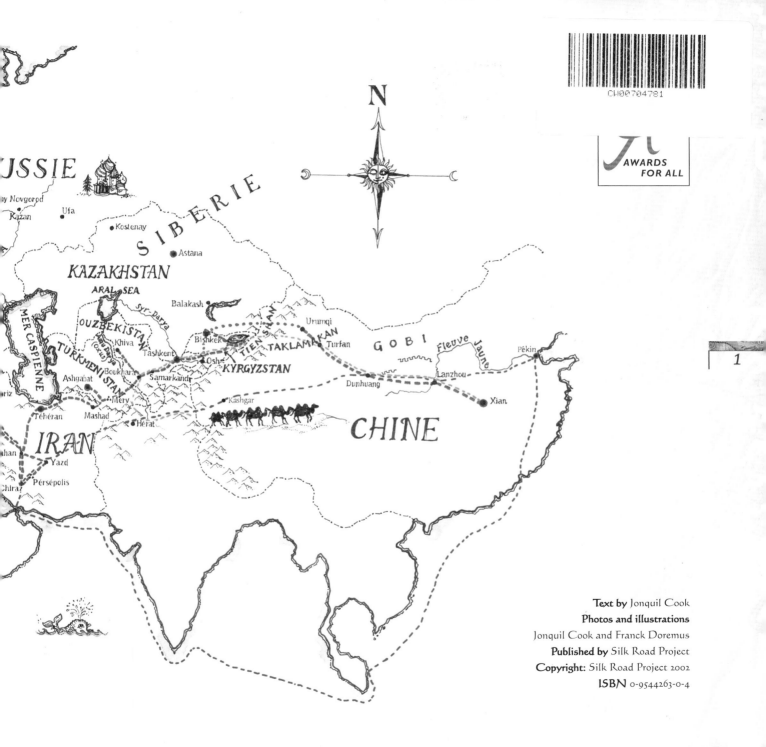

CU00704781

AWARDS FOR ALL

1

Text by Jonquil Cook
Photos and illustrations
Jonquil Cook and Franck Doremus
Published by Silk Road Project
Copyright: Silk Road Project 2002
ISBN 0-9544263-0-4

Contents

The tomb tower at Gonbad-e-Kavus, north-eastern Iran, was built by the poet and scholar, Ghabus ebn-e Vashmgir in the 11th century. This was of the only ancient monuments left standing by the attacking Mongol armies when they swept across Central Asia destroying almost everything in their path.

The Silk Road

For more than two thousand years man has been finding a way to travel the paths of the Silk Road. The result was the trade of goods: silks from China, perfume from Arabia, Indian spices and gems from Central Asia. Riding on donkeys, in great camel caravans, in LandRovers, even on foot, travellers have sought to bridge the gap, overland, between East and West.

At the end of the 13th century, the great traveller, Marco Polo, wrote his 'Tale of Wonders' about his experiences on the legendary Silk Road. The Chinese first travelled half way across Asia to connect with a route running from Central Asia to the Mediterranean more than one hundred years before Christ, but the Silk Road is considerably older than that, possibly by 2000 years or more. In the 7th century the Buddhist pilgrim, Xuanzang, travelled from Xian into India, via Central Asia, alone and on foot. It has been one of the greatest commercial passages in human history and a channel for the exchange of philosophies, culture and ideas.

Amongst the religions that played a part in shaping the character of the route, Buddhism and Islam had the strongest influences. However, many other religious movements such as Christianity, Shamanism, Taoism, Zoroastrianism, Manichaeism, Judaism, Mazdaism and Confucianism established themselves across Asia by way of this passage. The route passes through fabled cities and sites such as Babylon, Antioch, Baghdad, Bactra, Merv, Bukhara, Samarkand, Tashkent, Turfan, Dunhuang and Chang-an (Xian). Different branches of the Silk Road were followed according to the time of year, political climate or type of transport used, some through the north, others more southerly and some by sea. The term 'Silk Road' was actually coined by a European geographer, Ferdinand von Richthofen, as recently as the 19th century. However, the history, manufacture and story of how silk came to the West is symbolic of the cross-cultural links and exchange of skills and ideology that makes these ancient trade routes so important.

Expedition Landrover parked up next to yurts by the lake Song-Kul, Kyrgyzstan.

Lyon

Lyon was the last great European capital of silk production. Ever since the secret of sericulture was smuggled out of China, this place, at the meeting of the two rivers, is where the industry thrived in Europe. The alleyways and streets around Croix Rousse are still home to some of the countries finest 'canuts'. Some of the weavers, known as the Huguenots, demonstrated against the poor working conditions in 18th century Lyon and migrated to London where they set up workshops in the streets around old Spitalfields market.

At the Musée des Tissus we looked at examples from the archives of ancient, fragile silks and other textiles from countries and regions we would be visiting over the coming months: China, Central Asia, Persia and Turkey. These fabrics took our breath away with their beauty, intricacy and fine workmanship. We promised ourselves that we would seek out the modern equivalent of these designs in the countries of their making. At the CJ Bonnet silk factory in nearby Jujurieux, we looked at the great mechanical looms and learned a little about the history of the place, once famous for its rare black silk, supplied to a wealthy aristocracy that included Queen Victoria's Britain.

Silk looms on the factory floor of the soierie C.J.Bonnet, Jujurieux, France.

Bombyx Mori

Bombyx Mori is the name of the miraculous little creature whose sole mission in its very short life is to produce the fine silk filament. These little caterpillars grow incredibly fast feasting as they do on the leaves of the mulberry tree (nothing else will do, although various wild species of silkworm do feed on oak and cherry leaves: they produce a slightly thicker filament called 'Tussah' silk). The silkworm produces the filament in the cocoon spinning stage of its life cycle, but only if the conditions are favourable- i.e., warm, and with a plentiful supply of its favourite food.

'Sericulture', as the production of silk is called, originated in China at sometime around the third millennium BC. The discovery is attributed to the wife of the Emperor Huang-ti who, it is said, was drinking tea in her garden when a cocoon fell from the branches of a mulberry tree beneath which she sat. When the cocoon landed in her bowl of tea, Xi-ling-Shi('the Lady of the silkworm') discovered that the thread that unravelled could be stretched without breaking for more than half a mile. For centuries sericulture was kept a well-guarded secret and whilst travelling we heard several versions of the story of how the secret finally came to the West.

By the time silk had become an important trade item the Romans valued it more highly than gold. The sea passage between Asia and Europe became busy with freight, and Venice a port of increasing importance at the end of the Silk Road.

It was in Venice that we sought out the house of perhaps the greatest Silk Road explorer of all time, Marco Polo. Following in his footsteps we boarded a ship and travelled by sea across the Aegean…and into Asia.

1 The Bombyx-mori moth
2 Silkworm cocoons
3 The silkworm eating leaves of the mulberry tree

The Whirling Dervishes of the Mevlana cult.

Turkey

The minaret and fluted dome, tiled in blue faience, of the temple to Mevlana, source of the Whirling Dervish cult, in the city of Konya, southern Anatolia.

Ancient remains at the site of Ephesus on the west coast of Turkey.

On our arrival in Turkey we began our tour at the ruins of Ephesus, once the greatest city in Asia Minor, attracting the attention and envy of Kings Midas and Creosus amongst others. The Temple of Diana, nearby, was considered one of the Seven Wonders of the World. In the dazzling heat of the morning we walked amongst the polished marble and crumbling majesty of this once enormous city that once was home to a proud and cultured population of 220,000. We came across a Mulberry tree, and heard what would be the first of many tales and legends about how silk first arrived in this one-time great empire. The tour guides here tell that it is rumoured that a Chinese princess fell in love and came to Turkey to be married with a sultan's son. It seems that 'love' was the key in bringing the heavily guarded secret of the silk worm and its properties out of China. The princess hid a precious cocoon in the folds of her wedding garment, afraid that in leaving behind her home country she would no longer be able to wear her beautiful silk robes.

The city of Konya was once the capital of the Seljuk Sultanate of Rum, and, like Ephesus, also a remnant of a once great empire. The Seljuk Turks were at their most powerful and influential in the 11th century, the poet, Omar Khayyam, amongst their most noted emissaries.

Konya today is special for its remaining wonderful Seljuk architecture and the Mevlana temple and museum was a great example of this. Mevlana, also known as Celaleddin Rumi, was a great mystic of the Seljuk era responsible for the founding of a brotherhood called Mevlavi, the 'Whirling Dervishes'. In an ecstatic, prayer induced state the Mevlavi 'whirl', turning on the spot continuously for lengths of time without faltering. Watching them spin is a very beautiful and extraordinary thing. During the period in the early 20th century when ex-Turkish ruler, Mustafa Kemal (popularly known as Ataturk), sought to liberalise Turkey from the constraints of Islam, this movement was suppressed so that these brotherhoods now only exist in small numbers, dotted around Turkey and Syria. The beautiful mosque in Konya is a great testament to this fascinating form of worship.

Mosque in centre of courtyard in caravanserai at Sultanhani.

Heading east from Konya across vast, wide-open steppe country, a long, straight road between rolling plains of wind rippled grasses and fields of red earth led us to Sultanhani where we stopped to explore our first caravanserai. With no other visitors there to distract us we wandered around the stately, peaceful courtyard and surrounding chambers, imagining the huge, exhausted camel trains that would have stopped here for a few days rest after travelling for months across the unforgiving landscapes between here and China. These early versions of the 'motel', containing bathing quarters, stables, sleeping accommodation and a covered market place, were provided by the Seljuk State to encourage the safe passage and trade of goods along the Silk Road. Since leaving this first caravanserai we saw several more, in various states of ruin, at intervals of 30-40km along the road.

Caravanserai

Exterior of caravanserai at Sultanhani, Turkey

Archway surrounding interior
courtyard of caravanserai
at Sultanhani.

Sunday morning fishermen on the Galataseray bridge, spanning the Golden Horn.

Istanbul's Grand Bazaar ranks as one of the most famous market places in the world. Here, in the centre of the old city are elegant cloistered walkways with beautiful shops where carpets, silverware, antiques, textiles and painted ceramics are haggled over and bought by visitors from around the globe.

All around the extensive bazaar area are old buildings given over to shops and cafes that were once, also, caravanserais. It was in such a place as this that the wares of Xian and of the countries of the Silk Road were gathered together for sale to a European market.

Today this activity continues in the elegant little shopping street of the Arasta Bazaar. Here in the shadow of the Blue Mosque, upmarket shops sell antique textiles from Central Asia as well as from various parts of Turkey. Istanbul was, and still is, a major centre for the trade of goods from the countries we would be visiting.

Istanbul
Trading centre for the Silk Road

The Grand Bazaar, Istanbul

We were warned that this would probably be the last place along our route where we would find such a wealth of quality handcrafts from places such as Iran, Turkmenistan, Uzbekistan and Kyrgyzstan. We were shown gorgeous hand-woven "Ikat" silks from the 19th century, and older, hand embroidered pieces bearing tribal design. The rich colours, obtained from vegetable dye, are so different and subtle next to the chemically dyed fabrics, gaudy in comparison, made commercially today. Under Soviet rule the handcrafts of Central Asia almost completely died out to make way for industrialisation, and today the best pieces are scattered around the world, mostly in museums or private collections due to their scarcity. We would be lucky to find anything so valuable in the bazaars of Turkmenistan.

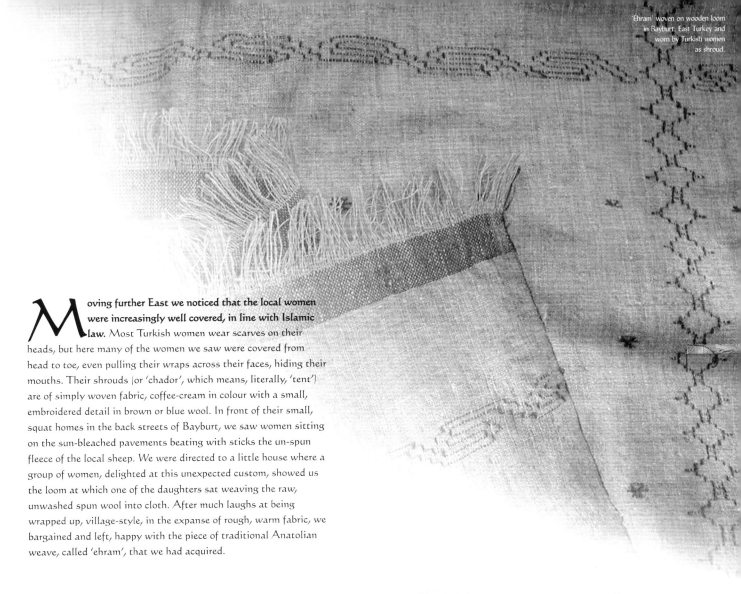

Moving further East we noticed that the local women were increasingly well covered, in line with Islamic law. Most Turkish women wear scarves on their heads, but here many of the women we saw were covered from head to toe, even pulling their wraps across their faces, hiding their mouths. Their shrouds (or 'chador', which means, literally, 'tent') are of simply woven fabric, coffee-cream in colour with a small, embroidered detail in brown or blue wool. In front of their small, squat homes in the back streets of Bayburt, we saw women sitting on the sun-bleached pavements beating with sticks the un-spun fleece of the local sheep. We were directed to a little house where a group of women, delighted at this unexpected custom, showed us the loom at which one of the daughters sat weaving the raw, unwashed spun wool into cloth. After much laughs at being wrapped up, village-style, in the expanse of rough, warm fabric, we bargained and left, happy with the piece of traditional Anatolian weave, called 'ehram', that we had acquired.

Eastern Turkey

Now in Iran, we found that Isfahan lives up to its reputation as the most beautiful city in the Islamic world. An oasis in the desert, full of beautiful gardens, tree-lined boulevards and some of the most stunningly beautiful architecture and mosques that we had yet seen. We found ourselves there at the hottest time of year, but eventually mastered the routine of an early rise and a morning of exploration, followed by a long and very necessary siesta. In Emam square we discovered most of the sights for which Isfahan is so special. The square itself one of the largest in the World surrounded by incredibly lovely buildings housing the colourful bazaar. This labyrinthine covered market is full of the best that Iran has to offer in the way of handicrafts as well as beautiful handmade carpets and the technicoloured array of spices for sale. Small back streets led to converted caravanserai and courtyards where artisans worked all day long hand printing cloth, weaving, painting fine miniatures on parchment and on smooth, lidded boxes carved from bone.

Iran: Isfahan

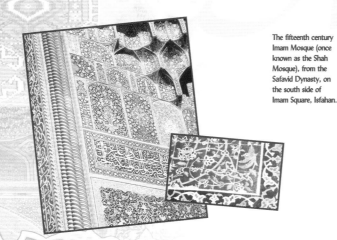

Details of decorative tile work from the Imam Mosque in Isfahan.

The fifteenth century Imam Mosque (once known as the Shah Mosque), from the Safavid Dynasty, on the south side of Imam Square, Isfahan.

We liked Isfahan so much that we decided to return here after our whirlwind trip through the Zagros Mountains to Shiraz and Persepolis in the south, and Yazd to the east. In the mountains we visited several tribes of nomads living in the valleys. We met families still living, separate from urban society, in their communities of black tent dwellings ('kara-chador'- meaning, 'black tent') and others who had been settled in barren villages with homes built of concrete blocks.

The Qashqai tribe is of Arabian origin, but their neighbours are Turks.

Qashqai Nomads
the Gabbeh

We spent a night with them, camped amongst red mountains covered with scrubby thorn bushes. The dairy animals provide the main source of sustenance for the tribe- sour milk with mountain thyme, fresh cheese and yoghurt and bitter white butter. So different from the city-dwelling Iranians, the women here dressed in fantastic colourful layers of splendid clothing: bright green, blue and yellow cotton with pink roses and silky textiles in every hue. In the shade of the tents, woven from the hair of goats, small looms lie on the ground and here- when their daily chores are completed- the women will sit and weave 'gabbeh'.

The 'gabbeh' is the carpet traditionally woven by the nomads of Iran. These are heavier and less finely knotted than the expensive, luxurious items to be found in the bazaars of Esfahan and Shiraz. The thick wool is spun by hand and dyed with the colours extracted from mountain herbs and flowers. The designs vary between tribes, but every carpet tells a story. Today the most popular carpets in the market places of Shiraz and Isfahan are almost figurative in design, depicting scenes of nomadic life.

The nomadic Qashqai people at their Summer camp in the Zagros Mountains, Iran.

Zohreh- a young member of a tribe of Qashqai nomads.

Backstreet in the clay-built desert city of Yazd, Iran. To the right of the picture can be seen one of the cooling 'wind-towers' that allow air to circulate between the baking walls and for which this city is reknowned.

The city of Shiraz was our base for a visit to the awe-inspiring ancient ruins of Persepolis. This was the great capital of Persia and royal seat of kings from 512 BC. Darius I and Xerxes both had palaces in their name in this magnificent complex.

At sunrise, before the tour buses arrived, walking alone amongst the gargantuan ruins, Persepolis was truly marvellous. It is debated as to whether the huge fire that destroyed the city in 331 BC under siege from Alexander the Great was actually sabotage, but it is easy to imagine that this great metropolis would have been the focus of much envy.

Persepolis and Yazd

Lions' heads and columns at the site of the remains of Persepolis, near Shiraz, south-west Iran.

Our next stop was Yazd, one of the oldest towns in the world, and we reached it through desert, along a desolate road swept with twisting, blinding mini cyclones and dust storms, traversing wide, flat, bleached white salt flats and scrub covered dunes. Everywhere we passed the mud-coloured ruins of crumbling caravannserai and ancient citadels. The old city is a labyrinth of smooth apricot walls concealing the adobe architecture where people still live and work- a living museum in the scorching southern desert.

Yazd was a key stop-off point for the caravans of the Silk Road, and a major silk-production centre for Iran. Marco Polo followed much the same route as we have done, visiting Shiraz and Yadz on his eastward journey. The road to Mashad, the holy city in the Northeast of Iran, cuts straight across this bleak, barren desert for hundreds of miles, but this was a part of the Silk Road that we chose not to follow at this, the height of summer. We did, however, spend our last few days in Iran in this most conservative of all Iranian cities: Mashhad is the holy pilgrimage site for the Shi'ite Islamic population who travel to that remote northeastern corner of the desert to worship at the shrine of Emam Reza.

Turkmenistan
the Tolkuchka Bazaar

We arrived in Ashgabad, the capital of Turkmenistan, during a thunderstorm that made the normally arid desert run with gushing brown rivers. This was quite unexpected: the apparently booming city looked to us like a cross between Vienna and Las Vegas with the exception that all the buildings of space-station-like proportions and design were built within the last few years. The effect is one of blinding white marble and enormous glittering fountains rising out of the desert like a science-fiction mirage.

On the edge of the Karakum (black sand) desert, which covers more than two thirds of this country, the temperatures at this time of year can reach 70 degrees centigrade and more. We rose with the sun and took a bus to the great Tolkuchka Bazaar- the most impressive and varied that Central Asia has to offer. On the fringes of the desert, under an already sweltering sky at 8 am, goods were laid out ranging from hand-woven textiles and antique jewellery to camels and car parts. Marco Polo commented on the amazing beauty of the Turkmen carpets he found here in the 13th century and 700 years later we too bore witness to a spectacle of colour and design such as we had never seen. The clothing of the Turkmen people, sheepskins and hand-woven silks in jewel-like colours, are beautiful. The Tekke tribe produce the most exquisite carpets as well as coats and hats of sheepskin and the finely embroidered 'chyrpy'. Although it was the people of the Salor tribe who were considered the best weavers, the Tekke were considered the finest textile artists. The 'chyrpy' looks like a long jacket but is in fact the traditional headgear of the Central Asian bride. In the wedding ceremony, the bride-to-be is blind-folded and dressed with heavy ornamental jewellery, over all of which is thrown the 'chyrpy' and the young woman is guided, sightless, by her female relatives, through a complex process of rituals. We found other beautifully embroidered items made by the people of the Yomut tribe, and found out that the carpets predominantly yellow in colour are made only by the Pendi people. Many of the Turkmen carpets sport a similar design, an angular motif called a 'gul', possibly influenced by the designs of Chinese and Sassanian silks that came to the region transported by Silk Road caravans.

Another explanation is that the design represents the 'kejebe' in which the newly wedded bride was carried on the back of a camel to her new home at the end of the wedding ceremony.

In the house of the master hatmaker, where camels munched on green hay in a shady courtyard, we were shown how the choice pieces of fleece are cut to make the woolly hats worn by the males of the Turkmen tribes.

We learnt that the sides of the sheep have the densest and softest wool while the backs tend to be barer and thin. 'Karakol' or 'Astrakhan' is the softest, finest and most sought after of all sheepskins. Silky, tight black curls used for the fashionable coats of rich women come from the tiny fleece of a lamb that will only drink of its mothers milk once before being slaughtered when less than a day old. Most skins used here to make the coats and hats we have seen come from sheep of less than one year old, those that have never been shorn. After shearing the wool becomes coarse and will then only be used for making felts and carpets.

We met Ludmilla Kiselyova, a batik artist, who works dying wool with chemicals in the carpet factory, but for her own work she uses plant dyes. Madder (marina) and aubergine for deep pinks and red; cochineal (from the carapace of a beetle) for sugar pink; indigo for every shade of blue and green; pomegranate for yellow and orange; walnuts for brown; onionskin for greenish-ochre and black from the seeds of a plant used in cleansing rituals. Colours vary for cotton, silk and for the wool she is using to make her own carpets. Her coloured threads are taken by the other craftswomen in the co-operative she works with and woven into the 12 inch strips of rough silk with the golden border that we found in the Tolkuchka Bazaar. These strips of cloth are then stitched together to make the colourful coats worn by the Turkmen.

13

1 The impressive sheepskin hats worn by the Turkmen elders for sale in the colourful Tolkuchka bazaar on the outskirts of Ashgabad, Turkmenistan.
2 One of the new structures that has changed the face of the city of Ashgabad since Turkmenistan's independence in 1991
3 Traditional Turkmen carpets for sale, and the wool used to produce them, at the Tolkuchka bazaar.
Background
   Embroidery on a 'chyrpy'. The young women of the nomadic Tekke Turkmen tribes wore these silk items as head coverings on special occasions.

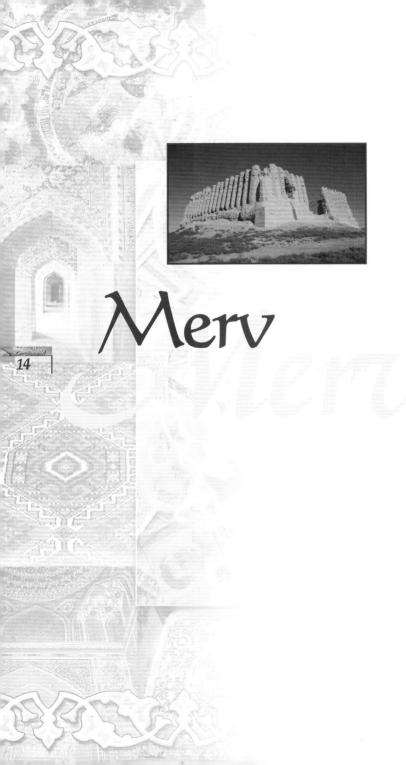

Merv

ear to the second largest city in Turkmenistan, Mary, we came across one of the most important sites in Silk Road history, Merv. It is probably 2500 years since the first buildings and walls of this huge city appeared, and the remains now cover an area of almost 100 square kilometres spread across savannah-like terrain.

Merv was known as the 'Queen of the ancient world', and its importance as a centre for trade and commerce was partly due to its positioning between several great nations including Persia, Afghanistan to the south, Central Asia and as a gateway to China and India in the East. In its days as a prosperous silk producing centre, Merv was surrounded by lush agricultural land, fed by the Amu Darya, or Oxus, River and was probably one of the richest and most beautiful cities to have existed. Over the centuries this great waterway, that has its beginnings in the Pamirs of Pakistan, changed its course and ceased to flow across Turkmenistan towards the Caspian Sea. It now flows north-westward to one of the World's greatest ecological disasters, the depleted Aral Sea. The land around Merv turned to arid desert and the crops began to fail. Then, in 1221, under Tuluy Khan, one of Ghengis' terrible sons, the Mongol armies razed beautiful Merv to the ground in about 15 days, murdering more men, women and children than died in the bomb-blast at Hiroshima.

Remains of the Great Citadel on the site of the ancient capital of Merv, Turkmenistan.

M erv, Bukhara, Khiva, Samarkand: these cities have conjured up more romantic images, evocative of the Silk Road, than anywhere else that we had planned to visit on our journey, and our expectations and ideals were far from disappointed. Equally, it was always the unexpected, found in back streets and in the homes of the kind people we met, that formulated the impressions and memories that we took away with us. Nowhere was this more evident than in Bukhara: the old city is unspoilt, lived-in and it feels as if time has stood still here. In the evenings old men wearing the traditional Uzbek skull-cap and long coats (called 'munisak') sit on raised platforms by a majestic pool known as Labi-Hauz, surrounded by ancient, gnarled mulberry trees sipping green tea and eating the local pilov (rice cooked with meat and vegetables).

The city of Samarkand was the jewel in the crown of the empire of Timur (or Tamerlane) and renowned as the 'mirror of the world' and 'the fourth paradise', but a series of earthquakes have wiped out most of the fabulous buildings that he had constructed. Many of these, including the Registan, Timur's mausoleum, the famous Registan, and the wonderful dilapidated Bibi Khanym mosque have been lovingly restored under the Soviets.

Of the many travel writers who have praised the beauty of this collection of buildings surrounding a great square, Ethel Mannin, in 'South to Samarkand' (1936) describes it beautifully: 'Facades, minarets, cupolas, archways- all are blue, delicate blue-green and deep pure cobalt. Moonlight mists it all to a pale softness, but in sunlight it is glitteringly brilliant, sea green, sky-blue, dazzling. Before the tiles began to fall away, leaving patches of yellow-brown clay, it must have been a flawless dream of beauty, but even in ruins it is the perfect introduction to the wonders of Samarkand'.

Uzbekistan
Bukhara, Khiva and Samarkand

In the shade of the Kalan Minaret marvellous, feisty little girls, aged between 8 and 14, mercilessly bombard the charmed tourists with their self-taught multi-lingual sales banter. At 47 metres tall, the minaret was once the execution tower from which the blood-crazed Khans of old would have their victims thrown to their deaths and smashed to pieces on the square below. The regions once ruled by Bukhara and by Khiva have an incredibly bloody and violent history, belied by the current sense of calm in the quiet, beautiful streets where crumbling medressas and mosques are decorated with gorgeous, jewel-like mosaic. 'Medressas' are Islamic institutions and, around the end of the 19th century, it is said that Bukhara boasted 103 making it one of the world's most important centres for Islam.

To visit Khiva, in the lush, green region of Khorazm where the Amu Darya begins to form a delta, we had to drive for several hours across the incredibly inhospitable Kyzylkum (red sands) desert. In its heyday, the slave market at Khiva was infamous and beneath the city walls we saw the damp, dark chambers where the hapless victims of the Turkoman slave traders would wait until sold. Today the city has been splendidly restored by UNESCO and has examples of the finest architecture we saw in Central Asia.

A sense of history is felt amongst the crumbling giants of the Bibi Khanym buildings- too big from the start to withstand the tremors in the earth. A difficult climb up a tower of the mosque rewards one with fantastic panoramic views across the city to the mountains bordering Tajikistan in the Southeast.

Timur's grandson, Ulugh-Bek, preferred the empirical truths of science to the preaching of the Koran. One of the most celebrated astronomers in history, he built a huge marble observatory on a hill outside of the city. We visited the site, where only the lower portion of the twin tracks supporting the giant sextant remain. Buried beside his grandfather, poor Ulugh-Bek was murdered by one of his own sons in 1449 for proposing possible alternatives to the words of the prophets.

1 Rooftop decoration in the ancient city of Khiva, restored by UNESCO.
2 The Islom-Huja minaret in Khiva, Uzbekistan.
3 Detail of the awesome collection of medressas and mosques at the Registan in Samarkand, Uzbekistan.
4 Mulberry tree by the Labi-hauz pool in the centre of old Bukhara.
5 Decorative portal to the 15th century Divanbegi Medressa, Bukhara.
Background
    Details of tile decoration at the Harem in Khiva, Uzbekistan.

From Tashkent we drove through a narrow neck of country, close to both the Kyrgyz and Tadjikistan borders, over the mountain pass and into the Ferghana Valley. Around 100 BC it was widely thought that very best horses for speed and endurance came from Ferghana and so much were they praised that the Chinese Emperor sent an army to obtain some. These were known as the 'heavenly horses'. The quest to find them brought about some of the earliest travelling on the Silk Road. We may never know what they looked like, but it may just be that some of these incredible horses do have descendants amongst the thoroughbreds of today.

The purpose of the Silk Route was to promote trade and create wealth. Today that trading fever is still apparent and the people who rely upon it are both the nomads and the settled farmers from areas surrounding the trading centres. Horses were just as much an important part of that trade as the silk and spices so very much desired in the West, and it was commonplace to trade horses for silk. A particularly fine horse would be worth a whole bale whereas a poorer specimen- perhaps only for consumption- would cost only a few yards.

The Ferghana Valley
and the Heavenly Horses

Participants of the Festival for Peace and Respect held in Osh, Kyrgyzstan, August 2000.

Akhal Teke horse, ancient ancestor of today's thoroughbred, in stables near Bokonbaev, Kyrgyzstan.

Kyrgyz horsemen in Osh, Kyrgyzstan.

Horses have always been abundant and important throughout Central Asia as trade, even during difficult political times, was always busy. With this trade was a constant flow of good livestock. The Emperor of China in 725 AD, in the 13th year of his administration, could count at least 430,000 horses in his herd. Camels were mainly used for cargo, horses for riding and warfare. The tenacious Turkomen, who inhabited large areas of Central Asia, were particularly skilled at selective breeding. They developed a horse that could not only climb mountains at a reasonable speed, but also sprint. Horses enabled the Turkomen to worry the Persians and the Russians to a considerable extent, constantly raiding and stealing women, valuables and children for the slave markets in Herat and Khiva.

The fearsome Mongol armies depended heavily upon horses in their conquest of most of Asia. For every soldier there would be five horses. This meant that the army could cover enormous distances very quickly changing horses frequently so that none grew too weary. It also meant that from afar the army appeared to be five times larger than it actually was, churning up great clouds of dust on the steppes that were seen for many miles and filling their victims with terror before they had even arrived.

The Yodgorlik
Silk Factory

Yodgorlik is just one of several NGOs that we visited after arriving in Central Asia, and the processes and difficulties involved in setting up and maintaining such projects in a region infamous for its chaotic bureaucracy became clear. We have been privileged in meeting and spending time with people of incredible devotion and determination in preserving the ancient handcrafts of these regions and maintaining them as fair trade profitable organisations. The factory was founded in 1984, during the Soviet era, for the purpose of reviving the production skills that were being lost due to mechanisation and commercialisation of the silk industry. Today a cheerful collective of men and women work on brightly painted looms producing the traditional, dazzling Ikat silks both for local use and export to the wealthy West. The fine, handmade pure silk scarves made for sale in America and Europe have been redesigned in subtle colour combinations and patterns to appeal to more conservative Western tastes. A British designer, Philippa Watkins, was brought in to work with the factory's own designer, Devlat, towards adapting the traditional Ikat, and increasing Yodgorlik's chances of commercial survival. At the same time, the electric colours and patterns favoured by the women throughout Uzbekistan continue to be produced using a silk warp but with a much cheaper synthetic thread for the weft. This allows the factory to produce affordable goods for the local market as well as those for exportation.

Young women workers at the Yodgorlik factory in Margilan, Uzbekistan, In the Ferghana valley, an area heavily industrialised during the Soviet era, local artisans are once more producing fine quality goods using entirely traditional methods. Yodgorlik is runas a non-government organisation (NGO) with assistance from the UN.

Ikat patterned silks on display in the showroom of the Yodgorlik factory in Margilan, Uzbekistan.

Stall selling Ikat silks in a Central Asian bazaar.

The roller pressing at the Yodgorlik factory is one of the few mechanised stages in the process of Ikat production.

Coloured silk warp threads waiting to be threaded onto a loom.

Ikat

The production of the Ikat we saw in Central Asia is complicated and made up of thirty-seven stages. Close to the factory in Margilan we visited a small co-operative where huge sack-loads of locally farmed silk cocoons are transformed into the spooled silk thread. The cocoons are sorted, washed, and then dropped into vats of boiling water to soften them. On a noisy production line in a small workshop, the women deftly extract one tiny filament of silk from each cocoon. Ten of these filaments are wound together onto a rotating mechanical frame to make a single strand, and then three of the strands are plied together and twisted to make one thread of strong silk. That makes thirty fibres in one silk thread. After spooling, the threads are hot washed for softening and strengthening and are now ready to be taken to the workshops at Yodgorlik. The next step in creating the Ikat is to prepare the warp threads that run lengthways on the looms. In both the pure silk and part silk versions of cloth, the warp is always of 100% silk. The 'davra' is a giant, rotating frame for winding and stretching the warp threads. Four hundred metres of threads are wrapped in a precise method around the frame ninety-nine times, fed by the spools, about one hundred of them, balancing nearby on tray of sand. After the warp threads have been removed, in strict order, from the davra, water is added once more to aid stretching and strengthening.

In his house in the quiet back streets we met Turgunbai Mirzahmedov, a master designer. Jailed for four years during a period of Soviet rule when independent artisans were outlawed, Turgunbai now ties and dyes the Ikat thread using his own, unique patterns, sitting on the shady terrace of his house. He pauses to pray before beginning to sketch the design on the bundles of warp threads spread out before him. In a little room off the central courtyard his young daughter, barefoot, works the loom and a kitten plays amongst the flowers on a sleepy, Uzbek afternoon. Back at Yodgorlik, the woven cloth has to be starched and ironed, ready for the shop floor or the local bazaar. The starching room has a very distinctive smell. The old man who works there fills his mouth with the milky, foul-smelling liquid and sprays it evenly and efficiently across the lengths of silk, his cheeks puffing. He is the 'spraying' master and responsible for the last but one process in the production of Ikat. On the other side of the courtyard men feed sections of silk through the enormous and rather dangerous looking roller presses, and pile them up, neatly folded, ready for sale.

Silk Ikat cloth being woven at the Yodgorlik factory in Uzbekistan.

Shyrdaks on display in Osh, Kyrgyzstan.

Women of the 'Altin-Oimok' co-operative in Bokonbaevo, Kyrgyzstan, dying hand-made felt using a traditional rolling technique.

Kyrgyzstan

Shyrdaks are the traditional felt carpets that line and decorate even the simplest of yurts, the traditional dwelling of nomadic peoples throughout Central Asia and Mongolia, and are unique to the little country of Kyrgyzstan, tucked away behind the Tien Shan mountains that separate Central Asia from China. Naryn is renowned for the production of the best quality shyrdak in the country.

'Ala-kis' are colourful carpets of pressed felt made in Central Asia.

The wool from the sheep of the Naryn River valley is rich in lanolin, thick, warm and perfect for the dying and pummelling that goes into making these incredibly beautiful felt items. Of the many lovely and varied designs we have come across along our route all seem to reflect or have their inspiration somewhere in the forms found in nature. In Kyrgyzstan the graphic, simple and elegant patterns definitively conjure up a sense of the mountains, the climate and the seasonally defined nomadic lifestyle. During the two months we spent here we took the opportunity to study closely the design forms that we had seen recurring in textile works since arriving in Asia. The ram's horn design is connected with ideas of wealth and power and when worked into the edging of a piece of textile is intended to ward off evil. The footprint of a bird signifies a blessing and happiness, and other symbols, such as the spiral form, simply signify friendship and unity. Much of this symbolic language had its roots in shamanism, a religious culture that still plays its part in the predominantly Muslim lives of the Kyrgyz, and has its source in the same region as that of the spoken Turkic language that resonates between the northern Steppe and Istanbul. From the carpet sellers of Turkey's 'Turquoise Coast' to the hawkers in the Central Asian bazaar we received enlightening explanations as to the meanings woven into the carpets and embroideries we looked at. Shown here are just a few examples of shapes and forms that once again seem to connect across the continents.

Our first real experience of this semi-nomadic lifestyle came about in the most stunning and majestic surroundings. Impossible to access without some serious wheels, we found ourselves at 3500 metres on the shores of glorious Song-Kul.

Here we parked up next to a small group of yurts owned by some shepherds, summering their herds of goat, cows, horses and sheep in the high pastures by the lake.

Tree of Life design

Ikat

Turkmen chyrpy

Uzbek mens' hat

Mountains

Rams Horn

Friendship

Horse tails

Examples of symbols used in design of 'shyrdak' and other textiles in Kyrgyzstan and throughout Central Asia.

View across the Naryn River Valley from mountains to the South-west of Kyrgyzstan.

Nomads

Along today's Silk Road it is still possible to encounter nomadic groups as we did in Eastern Turkey, Iran (the Qashqai tribe) and in the high mountains of Kyrgyzstan. Perhaps the most famous of all the travelling tribes that lived and traded throughout Central Asia were the Turkmen. Today the descendants of the Turkmen tribes that caused havoc across the steppes and far into what was then Persia are mostly sedentary, living in concrete dwellings on the outskirts of cities like Ashgabad. The Turkmen in particular were terrific horsemen and horse breeders, their pride in their animals clear from the ornate trappings of which examples can still be found. As a race their spirit was only quelled, after much bloodshed and loss of life on both sides, by the invading Russian armies towards the end of the 19th century.

With the development of governments, nomadism was discouraged as the central authorities found it necessary to keep track of the population. Amongst other factors, such as the development of technology and transport systems, this 'civilisation' of nomadic groups led to a gradual decline in the old caravanning traditions of the trade routes.

In the past, dependence on animals both for food and conveyance was crucial for man's survival. The Eskimo rode reindeer, used them for draft and ate them. The animals were both friend and meal, provider of clothing, and the means to sew it. No part of the reindeer was wasted.

Qashqai women at milking time.

We as city dwellers have come a long way from that level of survival. But the Indo-Europeans, the Persians, the Sythians, the Parthians, the Turks and all of the many tribes that have over the centuries peopled Central Asia, all of them needed mobility. The valleys and plains of the northern steppe, northern China and across the mountains westward were rich farming grounds for horse breeding and man needed the horse for survival.

Nomadic societies are more often than not people who have lived in settled farms but have been forced onto land that will not support year round grazing. It was these settled farms who learned to grow wheat and barley and to cull and develop animals to suit their lifestyles and taste. Today's nomads rely on the settled farmers for the grain to make their bread, just as the farmers and urbanites still depend on the nomads for their trade of foreign goods. It is the act of nomadism that encourages trade and was instrumental in the development of the great trading routes.

Nomadic tribes across Asia also favour distinctly different styles of accommodation. Whilst the objective remains the same, namely portability and shelter, the forms of these shelters vary greatly.

We have already mentioned the 'Kara-chador'- the black tents woven from goat hair- favoured by the nomads of Turkey, Kurdish country and Iran. Stretched wide and low across rough-hewn posts and braced with sturdy ropes, the fabric of the tents is weatherproofed using a smoking technique. Once the tent has been erected a fire is lit beneath of resinous pine needles, the thick black smoke of which encourages the fibres of the spun goat hair to interlock making it practically waterproof.

The yurt (a generic term for these domed dwellings) is predominantly the dwelling favoured by nomadic peoples throughout Central Asia and as far East as Mongolia. We saw our first examples of yurt in Turkmenistan, noticing the difference in shape (wider with lower roofs) from the higher domed 'boz-uui' of Kyrgyzstan. The Mongolian 'gers' are broader still with central posts supporting the roof.

CACSA

O ur primary concern whilst in Bishkek was in liasing with CACSA, the Central Asian Crafts Support Association, an umbrella organisation uniting artisans across the region and promoting their work on an international scale. The small but dedicated staff and team of volunteers are building on recent successes to reach more artisans in need of assistance, target new markets, enhance training programmes, lobby for artisans' rights on governmental levels, and develop other related projects. When we met the team, fronted by Dinara Chochunbaeva, they had been frantically busy preparing for a huge festival of arts and crafts taking place in the little town of Osh.

We flew to Osh and spent a week there, filming the events in the hope of producing a short promotional film for this dedicated and creative team. Back in the heat of the Ferghana valley, worked to capture the sounds and images of this colourful and magical event, entitled, appropriately under the current circumstances, 'Peace and Respect'. Performance artists and artisans from all the ex-Soviet countries, including Tadjikistan, gathered together under one banner and contributed to a week of entertainment, music and dance that the little city of Osh will remember for a long time. Also, in keeping with our, and CACSA's 'silk road' theme, some performers flew in from India adding to the amazing spectrum of colour and culture that intermingled.

Kyrgyz women wearing traditional dress at the Festival of Peace and Respect in Osh, Kyrgyzstan.

Issyk-Kul

The second largest alpine lake in the world after Titicaca, Issyk-Kul is an enormous expanse of clear blue water that never freezes even in the depth of winter (quite a feat at over 1500m). In the little village of Bokonbaevo we met with numerous artisans living and working in conjunction with a thriving farm co-operative, still productive and successful since the dissolution of the Soviet State. At the home of Sinbat, one of the women affiliated with the busy NGO, 'Altin Oimok' (Golden Thimble), we watched and filmed as villagers prepared thick, beautiful felt using age-old techniques alongside labour-saving, hand built machinery such as the mechanical roller press designed by Sinbat's husband. Felt making is a time consuming process. The wool is first beaten in order to clean it- something that can take up to a day to complete. Next the clean wool (either natural or dyed) is spread out in layers on a large mat of chi- straw that is also used as an insulating wall in the completed yurt. The weatherproof felt used for the roof and walls of the finished yurt is made up of three layers: white on the outsides and black in between. The chi, with the wool inside, is then rolled up and secured with ropes and then rolled and rolled (which is where the mechanical device has made such a difference to the workload) until the wool had been thoroughly compacted and flatted. Once unfurled, boiling water is sprinkled all over the wool until it is thoroughly soaked and then it is rolled up once more for further pummelling and rolling.

We sat down for tea (which is generally more of a banquet here in Central Asia and just as time consuming) in one of the yurts made from their own materials. We watched as the colourful shyrdaks were stitched together by hand, and felt was dyed using colour extracted from plants in enormous steaming vats beneath simple shelters. The 'Altin Oimok' co-operative is just about to move to a new location in the village, with better facilities, thanks to a donation and sponsorship from the US Peace Corps.

Constructing a yurt in the village of Bokonbaevo, near Issyk-Kul, Kyrgyzstan.

The great lake, Issyk Kyl (meaning 'warm lake' on account of it never freezing) lies at 1500m above sea level amongst the mountains of Kyrgyzstan.

Julduz Asanakunova masterminded the co-operative venture of building us our very own 'yurt' or 'boz-uui' to bring home to England. Sinbat and her family produced the amazing, thick, high quality felt which Kial, Nyrgyl and Gulnara worked on stitching together. Selkin, Julduz's mother in law, wove rope along with another woman from the mountains that produced 50 metres of rope for us from the hair of yaks. Zulaika, Umut, Guljan, Jypek and Anori produced the beautiful decoration- shyrdak panelling, woven strapping and the colourful chi.

With the help of the people that helped to make it we learnt how to erect the wooden 'carcas' with it's 65 'uuk' radiating from the central, giant 'tunduk'. The insulating 'kanat chi' panels encircling the wooden trellis-like walls ('kerege') are made from cut straw, decorated with coloured wool. The felt ('uzuk' on the roof and 'turduk' for the sides), tied down by woven woollen strappings called 'bors' is a sandwich of 3 layers, white on the outside and black in the middle. The wool comes from local sheep and is unwashed, the natural oils rendering the material almost weatherproof. Once the construction part was over, we set about decorating the interior with a wide panel of shyrdak designs, and an embroidered hanging that we acquired from a woman in nearby Kyzyl-Tuu, where the master maker of the 'carcas' also lives. The floor coverings are also of felt; the strongly contrasting and colourful cut-felt 'shyrdak', and the softer designs of the pressed felt 'ala-kis'. The 'tushuk' are long padded cushions, made of patchwork cloth and filled

Decorative stitched felt for a yurt made by Kyrgyz artisans.

with natural wool, for sitting or sleeping on and we lay them on the floor around the plastic tablecloth that was already laid ready for our 'yurt-warming' lunch. Before we left Bokonbaevo, Julduz presented us with 3 beautiful 'jurkan'; the jewel-coloured, velvety bedspreads that comprise most Kyrgyz women's wedding dowry.

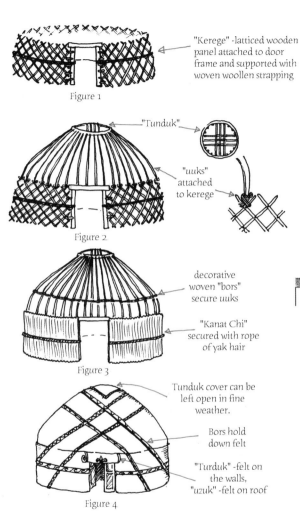

"Kerege" -latticed wooden panel attached to door frame and supported with woven woollen strapping

Figure 1

"Tunduk"

"uuks" attached to kerege

Figure 2

decorative woven "bors" secure uuks

"Kanat Chi" secured with rope of yak hair

Figure 3

Tunduk cover can be left open in fine weather.

Bors hold down felt

"Turduk" -felt on the walls, "uzuk" -felt on roof

Figure 4

How a yurt is constructed.

China: Xinjiang Province

The city of Urumqi was quite a surprise: shiny modern buildings and busy commercial areas- a big, thriving city on the fringes of the Taklamakan desert. Sparkling skyscrapers, straight lines and sharp edges; everything coated with a thick layer of wind blown sand and dust. Things were very different here- the sounds, smells, strange and colourful written characters, the people speeding past us in a sea of bicycles, bells tinkling. Nevertheless we were strongly aware of the fact that we had not yet left Central Asia behind us. Despite the modernity, there were still the chaotic, lively bazaars full of hawkers that looked far more European than Chinese. The women here wear colourful headscarves, with mouths full of gold teeth, and the familiar guttural sounds of the Turkic language we had been encountering for several thousand miles now ring in the air. Smiles for us on the street: 'jakshi' (good!) and 'rahmat' (thank you) worked here, too. The Uighur people make up around half of the population of Xinjiang at 7.2 million, the others being mostly Han Chinese.

Cooling wind-towers, similar to the kind seen in southern Iran, on the outskirts of Turfan, Xinjiang Province.

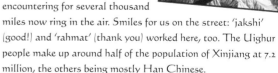

The T'ien Sha mountain ran that seperate China from t steppes of Central Asia a also known a the 'celestial mountains' o 'mountains o heaven'.

As with most of the tribes of Central Asia, the Uighur have their ancestral roots in Siberia, and having moved southwards, they were the first of the ancient Turkic peoples to settle. Their contact with Persian and Arab traders during the days when the Silk Road thrived in these areas, led to their conversion to Islam and eventually this form of religion overtook and obliterated the much older Buddhist following that had it's sources, also due to Silk Road trading, in India.

Turfan lies at 80 metres below sea level. Part of the Tarim Basin which lies between the southern and northern arms of the Tien Shan Mountains, the Turfan Depression is one of the hottest (up to 50 degrees C) and driest places in China. However, the town itself is an attractive, lush oasis, fed and watered using irrigation systems borrowed from the Persians. In lengths of up to 120km clay pipes, underground, carry cool melt-water from the mountains, beneath the scorched desert. Another cooling device that we recognised from the Iranian desert around Yazd, were the strange, square, brick constructed air-circulating structures that the people of Turfan build above their homes or stables to cool the rooms below. These were most noticeable on the outskirts of town, where we walked along narrow lanes to find the Emin Minaret- one of the most famed and recognisable landmarks on the Silk Road- standing surrounded by a sea of leafy vineyards.

Silk threads being extracted from cocoons using age-old traditional methods, in Turfan, Xinjiang Province.

The 44 metre high tower, patterned with sand coloured brick, reminded us of the Kalan minaret in Bukhara, so far away across the mountains to the west. In front of the building was the usual avenue of stalls selling tourist knick-knacks, but also, one selling hand woven silk.

Two men from Khotan, 600 miles south across the Taklamakan, sat spinning the thread in the old way, onto a wheel, with the cocoons bobbing in a vat of hot water. The designs of silk here are almost identical to those we saw in Uzbekistan- Ikat weave and colourful, electric patterns. The Ikat design cloth is the customary clothing for both men and women in closely related tribes, separated by a great mountain range and political territories. This was the only indication we saw that in some remote regions, silk was still being prepared in a traditional way in China.

Amongst the numerous archaeological sights to be found in China's Western deserts are the ruins of Jiaohe, once a great city 'between two rivers', thriving in this region 2000 years ago. The gorges that encircle the plateau on which the city was built are threaded with silver streams that sparkle between banks of abundant green, shaded by those great and familiar poplar trees that have marked our route since Turkey. Jiaohe is just one of a large number of sites 'discovered' by the first European archaeologists in the north western deserts from the mid-19th century onwards.

The Ethnological Museum of Berlin sent its first archaeological expedition to Turfan in 1902- the booty shipped back included 46 crates of antiquities. Later forays into the region resulted in the export of a further 34 tons sent back to Germany between 1905 and 1914 in a total of 387 crates. Sir Aurel Stein, the Anglicised Hungarian explorer, sent 141 crates to the British in India, all from the Turfan area.

Examples of this pre-Islamic Buddhist art had been preserved for 100s of years, buried under desert sands- and these explorers, perhaps well-meaning, perhaps just plain greedy, took it upon themselves to 'rescue' the priceless relics from a China that was, during the early 20th century, in utter chaos. One such highly respected scholar was Albert Von Le Coq, who was delighted and amazed at the discovery of about seventy cave temples at the ancient Bezeklik monastery 35 miles north east of Turfan. So much so, that he and his rather clumsy assistant chipped away the perfectly preserved wall paintings, with portraits of 9th century monks from a variety of places along the Silk Road: Indian, Asiatic and faces of a 'pronounced European type' with blue eyes and red hair. After 20 months of travel the paintings arrived safely in Berlin where, due to their great weight, they were cemented into the walls of the museum. Tragically, each and every one of them was destroyed when Allied bombs hit the building during WW2.

At the Mogao Caves, near Dunhuang, Stein was lucky again, when he succeed, along with the Frenchman, Paul Pelliot, in preserving for prosperity 1000's of priceless artefacts and manuscripts now on display in the Louvre and British Museum. Stein's 24 cases containing original manuscripts (including what is considered to be the world's oldest printed book, the 'Diamond Sutra', dated May 11th 868) cost him a mere £130. It is no wonder, then, that the Chinese government, now with it's own fabulous museums and centres for archaeological and ethnological research, would like these treasures back.

The route of the Silk Road that we were following passed through Dunhuang, Gansu Province, as it snaked north-westward towards the T'ien Shan. Here, where the Taklamakan desert meets the great Gobi, are some of the highest sand dunes in the World. Named the 'Singing Dunes' due to the strange sounds that emanate from them when the wind blows from a certain direction, we climbed them for great views across the town and seemingly endless desert.

The Great Wall

O n our way to Lanzhou we stopped for a bus-train connection at Jiayuguan where a great fortress marks the western limit of what is known as the Hexi Corridor. To the north are the wastelands of the Gobi desert, to the south the foothills of the mountains that rise up to the great Tibetan plateau. Whosoever controlled this passage, in effect controlled all operations and trade in and out of China. This was a key location on the Silk Road and much fought over. Close by, the furthest west remains of the Great Wall, winding up from the flat desert to snake dramatically across the sharp, black Mazong Mountains. This section was originally constructed during the 16th century; the wall presented us with yet another tough climb to more fantastic views…in the distance, the fort, and the snow-capped Qinling Mountains with tiny hilltop pagodas on the lower peaks.

"A tartar horn tugs at the north wind,
   Thistle Gate shines whiter than the stream,
      The sky swallows the road to Kokonor.
         On the Great Wall, a thousand miles of moonlight."
            –Li Ho, 'On the Frontier', 9th century.

Remnant of the Great Wall of China at its Westernmost point in Jiayuguan, Gansu Province.

Lanzhou

The city of Lanzhou and the Yellow River.

Duan Xinming is an award-winning caligraphy artist living and working in the city of Lanzhou, Gansu Province.

During our stay in Lanzhou, we were also privileged to meet one of China's most celebrated artists. Duan Xinming trained in the classical Western tradition of figurative painting; life drawing and realistic nature studies. Over the years his work returned to a form much closer to his Han Chinese roots, and now his massive paintings are of scenes that 'have their sources in the spirit, rather than the intellect'. Using the beautiful black ink of calligraphic artists, and the great, sweeping strokes from brushes with bristles made of wolf fur, he creates worlds in landscape on fine bamboo paper. He talked about the importance of relaying Chinese culture to the rest of the world, and this concept is more appropriate today than ever before. China, having finally opened its doors to the capitalist west, is at risk of losing it's ancient skills, philosophies and cultures once and for all now that the materialistic global culture threatens to homogenise us all. This rings true of so many of the artists we have encountered and talked with. There is a real risk that the crafts and traditions of so many ancient cultures will be reduced to the ranks of 'tourist fodder' with no real place in society. It seems that the responsibility for maintaining this cultural identity lies primarily with the artists and craftsmen of the world.

'Silk Road' written in an ancient chinese script.

Journey's End: Xian

Arriving by train in Xian we awoke to a grey dawn and the first sight of the great city walls, built during the Ming dynasty. This was our final destination and the source of the Silk Road itself. The first great capital of China, Xian was once called Chang'an and it thrived as a rich source of artistry under the highly creative Han and Tang dynasties.

The earliest known ink was made in China at least 2000 years ago. The first paper (soon to replace the beautiful but impractical 'papyrus' from Egypt) appeared in the 2nd century. The world's oldest known printed book- (the Diamond Sutra) was produced 600 years before Germany's Johann Gutenberg invented the printing press. Porcelain was made around 900 AD, but the technique that led to the production of 'china ware' in Germany was not adopted for another 800 years. More than 1000 years before the birth of Christ, the craftsmen of the Shang Dynasty were producing fine investment-cast bronzes with intricate, beautiful patterns in relief.

The ranks of statue warriors that comprise the great 'terracotta army' uncovered near Xian.

Statue marking the beginning of the Silk Road in Xian, China.

No visit to Xian would be complete without a visit to the world reknowned Terracotta Army. On the way to the site we passed the green hill that marks the tomb of one of the most feared and tyrannical of all the emperors in Ancient China's history. Mao Zedong himself is said to have been a great admirer of the Emperor Qin Shihuang, modelling his 'Cultural Revolution' upon the similar book-burning antics of his predecessor some 2,200 years later. So impressive was this Emperor of old that he had built this amazing and enormous 'army' to protect him where he lay entombed. The soldiers, some 6000 of them

(thus far uncovered) lined up in rank, stand 1.5 km to the east of the tomb, facing east- the direction of the rising sun and perhaps of Qin's greatest enemies. The army are an impressive sight- each figure entirely unique- cavalrymen, foot soldiers, archers, generals, horses and chariots. As well as those standing, there are uncovered sections, of the still only partly excavated site, where bodies lie broken, crushed by the weight of the earth above them. Their presence is as strong in this broken state as in 'life', like the aftermath of a horrific and bloody battle to defend the body of their Emperor.

One of our first quests in Xian was to find and visit the site that marks the very beginning of the Silk Road. We stood there, to the west of the city, in the driving rain, a large statue of a camel train looming above us. We felt a bit odd- anticlimax, perhaps. Here we were at the beginning, but it was the end of the road for us. We had been travelling for one hundred and fifty three days and now, having completed our quest, we were turning our heads, hearts and compasses towards home.

As we turned for home we began to trace a different route that the ancient Huns, Mongols and Tatars took as they, like us, braved the bitter northern winters on their way to conquer the West! Through history these peoples took part in and instigated events that led to the opening of passages along the network of Silk Roads. The Mongols, particularly, were responsible for the devastation of many of the spectacular ruins we had come across on our journey, but ultimately- in their successful quest for unification and the conquering of China- were the peoples that brought about the first real globalisation that the world has ever known. There has been an awful lot of bad press about Ghengis and his gang, but we are just beginning to understand how progressive and productive that extraordinary nation really was. It is said that in the days of Genghis Khan, a woman could walk alone along any part of the great caravan routes, carrying a bag of gold, unmolested. It is certainly not recommended today- particularly if you do not have the right paperwork!

MAY FIRST HOTEL XI'AN
长安五一饭店
长安中式快餐

MAY FIRST HOTEL XI'AN
长安五一饭店
长安中式快餐

The White Goose Pagoda one of the oldest building in the walled city of Xian.